THE FAMILY EXPERIENCE OF PDA

of related interest

**Can I tell you about Pathological
Demand Avoidance Syndrome?**
A guide for friends, family and professionals
Ruth Fidler and Phil Christie
Illustrations by Jonathon Powell
ISBN 978 1 84905 513 0
eISBN 978 0 85700 929 6
Part of the *Can I tell you about...?* series

**Pathological Demand Avoidance Syndrome
– My Daughter Is Not Naughty**
Jane Alison Sherwin
ISBN 978 1 84905 614 4
eISBN 978 1 78450 085 6

Helping Your Child with PDA Live a Happier Life
Alice Running
ISBN 978 1 78775 485 0
eISBN 978 1 78775 486 7

The PDA Paradox
The Highs and Lows of My Life on a Little-
Known Part of the Autism Spectrum
Harry Thompson
ISBN 978 1 78592 675 4
eISBN 978 1 78592 677 8

The Family Experience of PDA

An Illustrated Guide to Pathological Demand Avoidance

Eliza Fricker

Illustrated by Eliza Fricker
Foreword by Ruth Fidler

Jessica Kingsley Publishers
London and Philadelphia

First published in Great Britain in 2022 by Jessica Kingsley Publishers
An Hachette Company

12

Copyright © Eliza Fricker 2022
Foreword copyright © Ruth Fidler 2022

Front cover image source: Eliza Fricker

A CIP catalogue record for this title is available from the British
Library and the Library of Congress

ISBN 978 1 78775 677 9
eISBN 978 1 78775 678 6

Printed and bound in Great Britain by Clays Ltd, Elcograf S.p.A.

Jessica Kingsley Publishers' policy is to use papers that are natural,
renewable and recyclable products and made from wood grown
in sustainable forests. The logging and manufacturing processes
are expected to conform to the environmental regulations
of the country of origin.

Jessica Kingsley Publishers
Carmelite House
50 Victoria Embankment
London EC4Y 0DZ

www.jkp.com

The authorised representative in the EEA is Hachette Ireland, 8 Castlecourt
Centre, Dublin 15, D15 XTP3, Ireland (email: info@hbgi.ie)

This book is dedicated to B. I might have been a bigwig
designer, travelling the world selling international print designs
and furniture, I might have gone to parties and opening
nights and had weekends away, but instead I am here with
you, drawing, staring out the window and talking about the
pets, and that is fine with me. It is actually quite nice and
I will be here as long as you need me.

To Sherman for your voice of reason and those one-liners
it would take me weeks to formulate. You make me
feel sane in a mad world.

And lastly to Inca, our smelly old pug, who didn't manage
to make it to the end of the book. You had the breath of
a trawler man and minimal traits of an actual dog but
you brought so much calmness and silliness to our home.
You are missed every day.

CONTENTS

Foreword by Ruth Fidler

I was delighted when Eliza contacted me to share her thoughts about writing this book. Straight away it seemed to offer a different angle and a fresh format to the growing list of publications about pathological demand avoidance. PDA, as one of the autism profiles, shares other features of autism but is characterized by high anxiety, which in turn drives demand avoidance. That avoidance might be in response to demands that come from being asked directly or indirectly to do something, and can even derive from a person's desires to meet their own expectations or choices, which can at the very least be frustrating, and may also negatively impact on their emotional wellbeing or their self-esteem. It can impede their ability to learn, to participate or to flourish. Framing the book in the context of her experience of parenting her own daughter, Eliza blends honesty with positivity and gives all readers, but especially those who are parents or carers, guidance through a range of approaches that have been effective for her.

I have spent many years talking to all sorts of audiences about PDA, one of my personal fascinations and passions, but I don't always hear about how my key messages resonate with the audience. It was only when I first read Eliza's Introduction that I found out she had attended a talk I gave, and I'm so pleased that that experience helped her to understand her daughter's profile as well as contributed in some small way to the process of her producing this book.

I've always been motivated by understanding the young people I meet – getting to know their individualities and how they 'make sense' of their experiences, their networks, as well as becoming familiar with the character of their family. Using a combination of personal perspectives and drawings, Eliza's book helps anyone reading it to do just this.

Lots of families will find practical ideas, comfort and inspiration here. Extended family members, who often play key roles as aunts, uncles and grandparents not only in childcare but in supporting the family as a whole, will also find this book useful.

Children with PDA will be more regulated and resilient the more time they spend around other people who are too. Any of us, when in the midst of periods of difficulty, can find it hard to see a clear, wise path forwards. Families not only need support from each other but also from compassionate professionals who can provide encouragement and can help to spot progress and positives in a holistic way.

All of us can make a difference by protecting space for well-being and celebrating the small wins.

Eliza recognizes some of the challenges and exhaustion of parenting a child with a PDA profile. She shares, with honesty, the impact of how living with someone who can be anxious, impulsive and often unregulated can lead to other similar responses in the rest of the household. Under some of those pressures herself, it's no small feat for her to have found the time and energy to write this great book! While Eliza's book recognizes various complicated issues for young people and their families, one of its strengths is how she balances this awareness with the joys and freedoms to think creatively that are opened up by a greater appreciation of the PDA profile.

Eliza reminds us that we need to tune into the individuals we support, to approach them with an open mind and a warm heart. That just because they may not express their emotions the same way as others, doesn't mean they don't feel them. That just because we prioritize an issue one particular day, doesn't mean we have abandoned making progress, simply that the focus for right now needs to be elsewhere and we are taking a breath before deciding when and how to proceed. It means a very different style of parenting. Of course it does. Children who are developing in a distinctive way are bound to need a different approach. Embracing those differences means we can all thrive.

Ruth Fidler
Education consultant supporting complex
presentations of autism and wellbeing

Acknowledgements

Thank you to my always supportive husband; you do your bits and I do mine and it works. I really appreciate the early cups of tea and the morning dog walks you did so I could work first thing. And for feeding the cat too – I always forget about that.

Also Fran, Lucy, Laura, Kristy, Liz and all the other strong women I know who work so hard for their children and others.

Thanks to Emily and Ruth for your input on this project; it has meant a lot to me.

Introduction

I read a parenting book when I was pregnant and promised myself I wouldn't read one again. It just seemed like a reminder of how I was doing it all wrong, I wanted to read a book by a tired, flawed and contradictory individual, not a perfect parent who had it all sussed out, hour by hour, minute by minute.

I returned to the parenting section in the local bookshop again when our daughter started school and was still clingy, struggling at bedtimes and having meltdowns, but again most of them recommended time-out steps and strict rules and regulations, and that didn't feel right either.

My daughter was diagnosed with autism when she was seven. I went to a different section in the bookshop but even those books didn't quite resonate or ring true.

Years went by struggling with autism strategies at home and

school, such as routines, visual timetables and emotional scaling systems, but my daughter seemed to resist or reject most of these. We were floundering. Why were simple every-day expectations so hard for her? Why was she not allowing anyone to help her? It was around this time I attended a seminar day for girls and autism. There were various talks you could sign up for and I chose one called 'Girls Who Can't Help Won't', with Ruth Fidler, about pathological demand avoidance (PDA) and it all made sense; this was my 'lightbulb moment'. My funny, creative, sociable child was autistic but with such high levels of anxiety she avoided demands.

So I did go back to the bookshop (I do love books) and found a few titles on PDA and I learned more about what it was. I learned about meltdowns or shutdowns when the brain be-comes overloaded, masking, and the need for flexibility and autonomy. Our situation began to make a lot more sense to us.

When you have a child with extra needs you can often feel un-der more scrutiny, from other parents, professionals and even yourself. I know I felt this enormously when my child wasn't 'like the other autistic children' in school. I had a difficult time critiquing myself and my own parenting style. Was I parenting like this because I am a creative artist? Was it my upbringing? I was raised by artistic parents, while my husband was from a much more conventional, work-driven family. Had these two contradictory backgrounds created an enigma of a child? I scrutinized everything in those dark days.

I started to write and draw my experiences of parenting, partly to help me process it but also with the hope of connecting and resonating with other parents.

I drew comic strips as this is a genre of books I like to read and also because it allows for the nuances that are tricky to document in text; the subtle reactions or emotions and the environments around us. Comic strips are also accessible and easy to read and can be dipped in and out of – very important when we don't have much time on our hands!

So I wrote *The Family Experience of PDA* to help parents who are raising a child who is demand avoidant and to show how humour and compassion can help. It is really, really hard work parenting a child with PDA but it can also be good fun too. Humour plays such a huge role in not only supporting and connecting with your child, but also in relieving stress. Sometimes all we hear or talk about are the difficulties we face with our children, but our children can also be great company and I want to show all of this.

Parenting a child with PDA calls for empathy, kindness, calmness, compassion and humour, but it also requires connecting with other PDA parents because ultimately they 'get it'. They too are living it. When you are doing things quite differently from most parents and the societal norms or expectations, you need other parents who will back you up. Often instinctively, you know what is the best support for your child, you are doing it the best way for them but sometimes you will falter and question this. So you will need those other PDA parents who really understand that one teeth brushing a day is a big achievement or that you aimed to change the beds but sat down for a minute and fell asleep for two hours; that sometimes you are too tired, distracted or bored to pay attention to the specifications of every set of Bluetooth headphones and so don't know which model has the pull-out microphone; or that if every shop has sold out of the correct brand of malted wheat cereal, you feel a real sense of panic about how breakfast will go the next day.

Those professionals? Find those ones who 'get it' too. There are some really good ones, who want to support your family and who will work collaboratively to help you get the right support for your child.

Find them and hang on to them!

So here it is: my slightly funny, a bit flawed, quite tired guide to parenting a child with PDA as best we can.

Because that's all we can do; keep trying, keep learning and keep stockpiling the good sock resources.

I hope my book helps you, reassures you and makes you smile.

Keep going – our children might not always show it, but they need us. x

Tolerance Levels

Tolerance levels can fluctuate and change depending on other factors; in particular, if your child is already worrying about something then they will have a lot less capacity to deal with demands. So, it is important for us as parents to try and reduce the amount of demands we place on our PDA child. These can be anything from teeth brushing, to putting shoes on or deciding what to eat. A small change, but one that was significant in our house, was serving meals in a comfortable place such as on the sofa while watching television after a long day of demands at school. Your child may ask for something else to eat; this is not being fussy, this is because they are feeling very stressed and have a need for control in these times of anxiety, and that's okay too. We as parents just need to be as flexible and helpful as we can be when our children feel like this. We must be their safe person and place. Times like this are tough for everyone in the family, but even a demand avoidant child will have times when they are more relaxed and quite willing and want to help themselves.

These are the times when we will all be able to enjoy a joke together and we can jolly them into doing things.

As parents, we have to be masters at gauging our child's mood; some days they will be more flexible but at other times not want to do anything at all, and it's important to allow for these days too.

TOLERANCE LEVELS

HIGH

Clean your teeth please?

INCREASE DEMANDS _____ DECREASE DEMANDS

MEDIUM

Your toothbrush is loaded

INCREASE DEMANDS _____ DECREASE DEMANDS

I'll leave your toothbrush ready

LOW

INCREASE DEMANDS _____ DECREASE DEMANDS

The sensory issues such as taste, smell and touch as well as all the everyday expectations can lead to a child with PDA feeling overwhelmed. Everyday demands may seem too much for them. The anxiety may also be higher or lower on different days and means that the child's tolerance levels are higher or lower.

Minimizing the demands and helping your child get ready can really help to prevent their brain from becoming too overloaded. My daughter would hate us to 'fuss' and get her dressed so now we put her clothes out ready on the bed and 'load' her toothbrush. We use indirect language like this to also take away the 'demand' and keep our tone of voice as even as we can.

How the brain can become overloaded

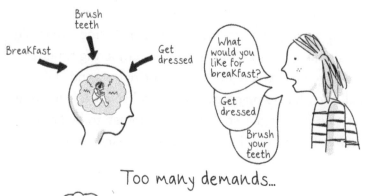

Too many demands...

Combined with sensory issues such as smell...

Taste...

It is always a juggling act, making sure one pair of wearable socks she likes is always available, remembering timetable changes, going to the right shop for the right brand of cereal and all the while remaining calm and collected. It is definitely not always possible, so if the teeth 'forget' to be brushed some/most mornings, just aim for bedtime instead!

Touch...

and the sequence of doing things

Can cause the brain to overload...

Leading to meltdowns...

How to keep the brain neutral

being as discreet as possible

Take away the need to make decisions

Remove any pressure or demand

Five minutes later

Avoid eye contact

Use indirect language

Meltdowns

Meltdowns are not temper tantrums. They are an indication that the brain is overloaded. They happen when a child can no longer cope. They can be explosive or implosive, with the child sometimes lashing out and at other times shutting down or hiding away. This is the flight or fight response. This is not a time for discipline, threats, rewards or sanctions. The child has lost control and the brain needs time to reset itself. It is important to make sure they are safe but then keep communication to a minimum.

Time is everything; you may be late for where you are going, and you may not be able to do what you planned to do, but none of this matters as the most important thing is to support your child by staying as emotionally stable and level as you can.

They will be calm again and it will be over a lot quicker if you are not upset or angry with them. The meltdown is not related to your relationship with your child or a result of you not being a good enough parent. Their brain is wired differently and you are seeing a result of this. Your child is not doing it on purpose. Once we as parents can see beyond the behaviour, our empathy increases and we will feel able to help our child. It is a good idea to have a think afterwards to see if you could have done anything differently.

Did you put too many demands or expectations on your child?

It has taken me several years to integrate this way of being as a parent. It takes time but it can become part of how you parent, and there is always time to change or adjust how you do things.

Switches on

'The Look'

Go to other room

Twenty minutes later...

Head towards bedroom...

Distraction after the meltdown is the best way forward. Our daughter doesn't want to talk about it; she just wants to move on. I clean up any mess she has made and then divert her to something else. When I stay calm I always feel that the meltdowns end more quickly and afterwards I don't feel racked with guilt for shouting either! But we are humans with feelings and stresses of our own and this won't always be possible, so give yourself a break when it doesn't go to plan!

You can help your child understand emotions but find a calm and different time to talk. Avoid doing this straight after the event when you are all still feeling a bit sensitive. A child who is demand avoidant will find talking about emotions difficult, so picking a time when they are relaxed, such as when you are walking, can be good – when you are side by side and not face to face can work really well. You can even talk about yourself and things you find difficult and how you deal with them; then the onus is not on your child and this removes any expectation. You can add humour to this too. Try and make emotional and social learning as relaxed as you can so your anxious child does not feel expectations on them. The PDA child is highly sensitive to criticism, so you need to make learning and discussions more general and refrain from putting emphasis on their behaviour.

A PDA child will do well if they can, but they don't do well if they cannot live up to demands or expectations. We can work together with our children by supporting them and seeing beyond the behaviour.

Relationships

PDA children can gain a huge amount from positive relationships. These are key to children navigating a better social and emotional understanding. My daughter gravitates towards a few people and these tend to be natural, relaxed and funny personalities. Often positive relationships for a PDA child will work as well or more effectively than any other support structures. The child can gain a lot from these relationships and they will help them to navigate situations as well as support their anxiety.

PDA children are drawn to 'natural' people: those who are relaxed and laid back with children, as well as those who demonstrate that they like and respect them. Our daughter will not tolerate even a slight condescension or authoritative tone of voice and is very adept at picking up if someone is slightly uncomfortable around her. She will decide whether she likes a person very early on and it will be unlikely that her view will alter.

She struggles to differentiate the hierarchies and does not respond well to authoritative figures, as these are likely to place more demands on her. I remember her getting extremely upset when she was 'told off' and I am still careful to decide whether this is ever necessary. This means that often my role as mum is more in the style of a friend to her.

RELATIONSHIPS

She shows affection in different ways

There are lots of misconceptions around feelings and autism, particularly when it comes to affection and love. Autistic people do have feelings and emotions like everyone else but may express them differently. I have never had a hug, kiss or been told I'm loved by my daughter. For years I used to feel sad watching the other parents at the school gates as their children ran up to them for hugs and kisses. But then I thought about it differently, and realized that since my daughter is very particular about who she lets into her life, I am very lucky that I am one of the 'chosen ones'. I do feel loved by her, she just shows it in different ways and it also makes these moments *our* moments, and so they feel extra special to me.

We have our own ways...

A little smile...

I never get kisses or cuddles but my attention is not totally rebuffed

Autism and PDA present in as many diverse ways as any other human characteristic. Even with a diagnosis, a PDA child is still a product of their environment, upbringing and parents. Our daughter is creative like me and a good problem solver like my husband.

However, PDA children tend to appear more sociable than many children with autism. My daughter has several close friendships and these are essential to her. They are her motivation to leave the house and to engage in activities.

She has known these children a long time and they are accepting of her ways, such as when she may abruptly want to go home if she has had enough.

They can also be intense friendships that she finds difficult to allow other children to join in with, but as she has got older she is getting better at managing this. Being around our friends has helped with this too as she very much takes her cues from her key relationships.

As her parents, we encourage her friendships and the independence these give her.

friendships

Good friends understand when she has had enough

When the PDA child is demand avoidant, the expectations of the school environment can be very difficult for them. Even when a child is bright and creative the classroom setting can be overwhelming. Usual classroom practice means that teachers put lots of demands on all the children, all the time, and there will be much expectation to try to do things correctly.

For our daughter, friendships, as well as certain staff members, were key to her engagement at school. A good teacher or teaching assistant for a PDA child will know how to interact in a natural way, using subtle distraction when the child transitions into school in the morning. If the child is feeling overwhelmed they will pick up on the little changes in the child before they have a meltdown or shutdown and they will play games while having conversations to improve their social skills.

These relationships made the difference as to whether my daughter was able to go to school, so, as well as being invaluable to our daughter, they have been invaluable to us too!

The PDA child is nuanced at picking up on patronizing, loud or exaggerated tones of voice

A calm and unflappable teaching assistant is worth their weight in gold...

Who uses subtle distraction techniques

And is around when they need a break .

Sensory Needs

PDA is best understood as part of the autism spectrum, so, like other children with autism, children with PDA will often have difficulty processing sensory information. This can be connected to touch, hearing, taste, smell and sight as well as internal senses of body awareness (proprioception) and movement (vestibular).

The brain can struggle to process all the information and can create conflicting signals. This can lead to different behaviours, meltdowns or shutdowns so it is important to recognize what could be tricky for your child.

Sensory issues can be heightened at times and tolerance levels can fluctuate when your child is feeling particularly anxious.

Sensory

Needs

Clothes can be tricky to navigate; in our house, wearing socks is really difficult. There are so many variables to them; they have seams, they can get rucked or squashed in shoes, and they need to be washed regularly and this will cause them to feel different.

So we try to buy lots of the same socks and will let our daughter wear her favourite pair numerous times before going through the ordeal of washing them.

I always try and weigh up this tricky situation and decide whether it will make an anxious time, such as getting dressed, leaving the house, getting in the car or meeting people, less stressful for everyone if she can wear grubby socks. We get to leave the house rather than not and I don't think anyone has ever died from wearing dirty socks!

We have spent a lot of money over the years on different clothes that have never been worn and dread shops not stocking favourite items anymore. We try to buy lots of the same t-shirts and shorts and underwear. We cut out the labels and make sure to wash clothes before she wears them too.

A few minutes later...

Seasonal changes mean a change of clothing. Coats, hats and gloves in winter are often woolly and bulky and so are never worn.

Keeping clothes the same and predictable helps keep the anxiety levels down.

The same can also be said for food. Often it is the consistency of flavour that only branded foods can offer that works best. This food is also often bland and can be more palatable to a child who finds that smells and tastes are heightened for them.

Some children can even tell if it is a different brand of cereal or crisps to their usual one. So in our house we try to keep to the same shops and keep stocked up on favourite foods.

Hunger can be a big contributing factor to meltdowns in our house and so it's best not to wait until your child is really hungry because they can find making any decision about what to eat when they are hungry really difficult.

The mornings can be tricky anyway as the home may be busy with everyone getting ready, and this combines with apprehension of the day ahead. We often just put a favourite breakfast down in front of our child and leave her to eat it when she's ready.

At school, her favourite teaching assistant always keeps a packet of biscuits handy for those low blood sugar moments when our daughter may have not eaten breakfast or be start-ing to flag mid-morning.

Some children can be sensitive to noise and will like to wear headphones to cancel out external noise, and PDA children may prefer earphones as these are subtler and therefore do not draw attention to them or make them stand out.

Our daughter likes to wear headphones to watch videos on her phone to keep her calm. She doesn't mind noise and quite likes busy places.

The pier where we live is great for our daughter as she craves the input this gives her when on a fairground ride.

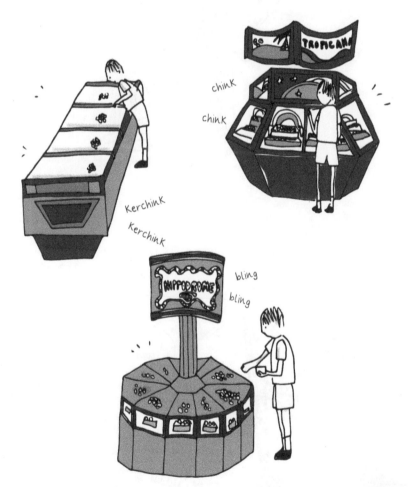

chink

chink

Kerchink

Kerchink

bling

bling

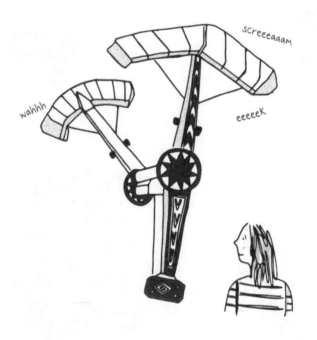

You will know your child best and what works for them. This can fluctuate on different days and weeks, and sometimes conflict or be quite contradictory with what worked previously.

Sensory toys can be used to help a child relax, such as a squishy or fidget toys. It is really nice for others to also embrace something your child loves, which could be a takeaway from their favourite burger place or saving up lots of loose change for an afternoon on the slot machines. Doing something they really love can be a big incentive to get out of the house and have fun. But they may decide it is too much (as in too much demand) and they can't go out, so think creatively – even rolling up in a duvet and then unrolling can be great fun for them!

Anxiety

For our daughter, anxiety is at the forefront of most of her daily life. It is so overriding it can mean she will avoid doing something, even an activity she likes doing. Sensory issues combined with the demand of doing something will likely increase anxiety. There can be many variables involved in doing an activity too, such as how to get there, the change in routine, as well as unpredictable events like the bus being late or somewhere being too busy. The pressure of expectation or demand can also be too much, and this can come from other people or herself. Our daughter struggles to leave the house; sometimes we get to go out but we have also been late or not gone at all as she has been too overwhelmed. This means that when we are going out I can feel anxious too as I am worried we won't get to go. I didn't start out as an anxious parent but I became one! So I have had to become very aware of myself and try to remain calm (or at least appear calm!).

If another family member is really looking forward to doing

something or the PDA child might have shown an interest in going to the cinema last time they went, there are now expectations. This is when their anxiety can take over as there are too many demands and expectations, the child becomes very anxious and their brain becomes overloaded, leading to a meltdown or shutdown.

The PDA child's brain can become overloaded or overwhelmed very quickly and this leads to a fight or flight response.

Anxiety for the PDA child can be debilitating and can show itself in many ways. They may use a variety of distractions to delay doing something; they may ignore you, or argue or even incapacitate themselves. When our daughter is in uncomfortable environments or with people she doesn't know, she can seem almost serenely calm but this is her going into freeze mode. She will look completely blank and this will result in her being sick if she can't remove herself from the situation. This is her anxiety attack and it is very unlikely she will feel comfortable to go back to a place where this has happened as she has felt extreme stress at this point. For her, feeling trapped is terrifying and it is important that she feels she can remove herself to a safe space when she needs to.

Flight, fight, freeze, fawn, flop, fluster, flock are the body's responses to fear and the PDA child may react in any of these ways. As their parent, you will probably be astute at recognizing these, but others may not be, so it can be really helpful to make people who are looking after your child aware of potential triggers and what the responses can look like.

Remembering anxiety is at the forefront for a PDA child is really important so we can remain compassionate, kind and calm to help our child.

It can be disappointing and frustrating when we have something planned or need to leave the house at a certain time and then this doesn't happen, but we have to try and remember that their anxiety levels are often so high that it is preventing them from doing something. It can also be difficult for siblings who miss out on days out or are late getting somewhere, and as parents we might not get to see friends or spend time together as a couple. I know we have lost lots of days out or come home early. This is disappointing but we do not want our daughter to feel guilty on top of her anxiety. She is really sensitive and we wouldn't gain anything from making her feel bad on top of how she is already feeling.

It can also be puzzling for us when they refuse to do something they want or love to do, but, remember, the demand or expectation to do it for themselves or for others can just add too much pressure. This is also not the time to say, 'But you love going...' or, 'But I've just signed you up for 12 drum sessions and it has cost me a fortune', as this will create more expectation on the already anxious child. It does matter to us and it can be hugely disappointing to all the family as well as extremely costly in wasted money, but we are only making things worse for them by letting them know this. *So, no sighing or arm-folding either – they are astute at picking up nuances in our behaviour!* Having a chat about it at another time, when they are calm, is helpful. I will 'drip feed' to my daughter before I have to go somewhere by saying that it will be good for work or will make her dad happy rather than it is really important.

Transitions are always tricky in our house. At home, we keep demands and expectations low for our daughter and this means she is often a lot more able to do things such as get her own drink or snacks (on a good day!) or have a bath (eventually/maybe!). Transitions vary – if our daughter needs to leave the house to go somewhere, it is harder if she is going somewhere she has not been before. We try not to add too many new elements to this. We may choose to drive so she doesn't have to also comprehend a new bus or train route and we will keep dialogue to a minimum so as not to overload her. We will refrain from asking her too many questions, such as, 'Do you want to take a drink?', and just put a drink in her bag.

Another scenario could be a family member going out or all of us going out so that someone may be coming to our house to look after our daughter. All of these are transitions for our daughter. She doesn't like visual timetables as she sees these as demands, so we use a drip-feed technique to gently remind her. We 'drop' these reminders in for a few days before. Our daughter is also very forgetful so we have to do this several times or she may forget and get distressed – but not too many times or it will become a demand for her. Home is safe and mostly predictable, but going out and the transition of getting out can be difficult. Giving plenty of time to get ready is important and allows for difficulties with all the potential tricky bits such as socks, shoes and so on. Also, if teeth don't get brushed, try not to worry, aim for before bed instead; and if breakfast doesn't get eaten, put some biscuits in your bag for later. Much of their emotional regulation comes from their trusted adult, so if you are relaxed, they will relax.

This is not always easy and we will all have our own emotions as well as stresses and strains happening while appearing as Zen masters to our children, so it is important to take time out for ourselves. Often it feels as if we have to be perfect for our children and this is not possible. It can and does take its toll at times and I have found getting to know other parents of PDA children has been really helpful as they 'get it'. Everyone in the family has to make sacrifices and that is hard on all of them, so it is important we all take a break, either siblings alone with parents or parents as a couple, or just on our own. We have an elderly dog that walks very slowly and these slow dog walks round the neighbourhood staring into space have kept me sane!

ANXIETY

Don't rush them, even if they are stalling

Our daughter often uses various stalling measures such as needing to find specific things, but she is actually using this time to mentally prepare herself. We need to give her this time and not rush her, otherwise her anxiety levels will increase and this will lead to a shutdown or meltdown, and then it will be very difficult to get her back to a place where she will want to resume doing the activity.

It is important for our children to feel in control. Anxiety and autonomy go hand in hand in our house. If our daughter feels in control and is able to make choices, this reduces the anxiety. As long as the child is not doing anything that is a threat to themselves or others and they are safe and not hurting anyone, then they can be in control or feel in control.

It is difficult to unpick what causes their anxiety because direct conversation can make them very uncomfortable, but doing activities your child likes when they want to do them is really helpful to them. It regulates them and makes them feel calmer. Often this is a time you are not using direct eye contact and so your child will be feeling most relaxed.

Sharing your experiences can be a good way to help them feel more comfortable about talking about their tricky situations.

Finding activities I know she likes can have
a really calming effect
If there is something bothering her she is
more likely to chat when relaxed and safe

Collaboration

I like this word! When you have a child with complex needs it can be overwhelming at times and even difficult to see beyond the behaviour. So words that are immediately constructive and positive surrounding PDA and that help support your child are ones I always latch on to! Collaborative approaches are also really important between adults with a PDA child, whether this is parents, extended family or professionals.

Demand avoidance combined with anxiety means that if there is a task or something you need them to do you will need creative ways to present it to them.

For example, if I said my daughter's name and then, 'We need to leave the house to buy milk and bread' or, 'Can you put your shoes on? We have to go out and buy some milk and bread' these would be very clear and direct demands I was making of my daughter. Even if I had made a timetable with Wednesday as the day to go out and buy groceries then I would have created an expectation that Wednesday is a day to go shopping and an expectation that my daughter does this. I may have a calendar myself but I don't use one for my daughter (and I am always well prepared for my calendar to be as flexible as it can be!).

So instead of asking or telling my daughter to do something, I use a collaborative approach instead.

A collaborative approach is a way of working with your child to come up with plans together. You are reaching a decision about a task that needs doing together by using indirect language – by suggesting what needs to be done you are giving your child the autonomy to come to the desired outcome. I also try to continue to keep the conversation to a minimum at these times to avoid overloading my daughter, and I give lots of processing time too.

This may seem an unnatural way of communicating at first, or different from how you communicate with your other children, while for others it may not be a million miles away from how you already communicate with your child.

For me, it has been a gradual learning process and response over a number of years (with some massive errors along the way!) to really embed it into my way of thinking and the dialogue I use, and now, several years down the line, it almost (!) comes naturally.

I also enjoy it as our interactions are so much less combative and therefore make for a more pleasurable and calmer home.

A little while later...

Collaborative ways to communicate.
Best used with minimal eye contact
and side on...

My daughter also really enjoys feeling useful and purposeful, so if she has been engrossed in computer gaming or her phone too long, then I might do something ineptly near her and she will enjoy helping me or rectifying my mistake.

These are great bonding times too. My daughter loves seeing me messing around or making mistakes (deliberate or not!) and it's a good way to change the mood. This collaborative way of being with your child removes the traditional hierarchy in the relationship of the parent and child where perhaps as a parent you may put demands or expectations on your child to do certain things and behave a certain way. The collaborative approach is a way of getting a few manageable things done so that your child still feels in control and therefore is a lot less anxious.

Fun

Fun is my gateway in. Fun is my secret weapon. If I could only have one supply or one skill forever it would be fun! This is not only where my most positive outcomes result from, it also makes me feel a lot better too.

What makes you feel good? Laughing? Smiling? These things make us feel lighter, less burdened and less anxious. A good friend or partner who knows how to make you laugh is often just what you need. So for your PDA child, who feels very anxious a lot of the time, this can also be a perfect tonic.

Fun is a really good icebreaker and my daughter judges lots of her relationships and friendships on who has a good sense of humour or who can see the funny side in themselves. These people are going to be more relaxed and in turn place fewer demands on her.

One of her favourite people is my mum because she is very

natural and relaxed around children, does not see any adult/ child hierarchies and is also happy to appear incompetent whenever needed!

In fact, even as a grown woman I'm not sure how much she is actually putting on an act, but it is really funny and makes me and my daughter laugh.

Slapstick humour is a great diffuser of potentially stressful situations or if I am struggling to get my daughter to engage with me.

Using a bit of silliness and being able to show your child that we all make mistakes is also a really positive way for them to see it's okay if you get things wrong. We all make mistakes and that's all right. So your PDA child will probably gravitate towards the natural, funny people in their life. I have found it great for us as a family, and the more laughter the better. It makes me feel better as a person and as a mother too (being a parent to a PDA child is really tough at times!).

If being humorous doesn't come easily to you then you can watch funny television programmes together. We had a TV series we all liked for a while and my daughter would want to watch an episode before bed. This was a nice end to the day too and would eradicate any stress accumulated from school and home. Sometimes funny scenes from favourite comedies can also provide reference points for conversations when things happen in real life too.

I have found that humour has also helped other family members who have not been as comfortable or as able to relax. When they see us mucking around and joking they see it is okay to be relaxed and silly too. Family will worry about you and all you have to juggle, so it is good for them to see there are nice bits too.

But remember, being fun is sometimes hard to do, especially when you are tired or stressed, so making time for yourself in adult company and being a grown up is important too!

FUN

Being fun can be tiring so make time
for yourself to rejuvenate too

Flexibility

Over the years, I have had similar conversations with a variety of people who have spent time with my daughter and they have often been along the lines of, 'Does she not like doing...anymore?' 'She used to like...and now she doesn't'. I have also had the same confused conversation with myself. My daughter will seem to be really enjoying a hobby or activity and I might start to engage with this new interest too. I might show this by asking her questions and talking about it with her, I might go and buy something to help with the new hobby or I might chat to a family member and share my enthusiasm that she has found a new hobby so enjoyable. However, after a number of hours, days or even weeks my daughter will lose interest in the new hobby.

I have been left confused at this sudden refusal to engage with the new hobby that she seemed to enjoy. How could she like doing something so much one day and not the next? It has also been disappointing as I have really wanted to find something that my daughter enjoys, something that might get her out of the house for a few hours or create a welcome break from spending time on a screen. I am hopeful that she can share this new interest with her teaching assistant at school and it could be something for them to do together. However, this often abrupt end to an interest is very common because I have shown my daughter my perceived expectations, I have shared this with family or teachers and they have in turn shown their enthusiasm too, and in doing so we have created a lot of implied demand.

FLEXIBILITY

Later on that evening...

A few days later...

Buying a book, or even just talking about the hobby, can imply an expectation on our child that we would like them to do more of their new interest.

You child may talk enthusiastically about their newfound interest but keeping your response as low key as possible with a brief response such as 'great' or 'sounds good' will minimize the perceived expectation.

If you can keep autonomy, freedom and flexibility at the forefront then your child can feel as if they are accessing their chosen activities at their own volition.

Sometimes a PDA child will find even their own demands to do something too overwhelming. It's not that they don't want to do something, but it's the perceived expectation or demand on themselves that makes it too difficult to do that favourite activity, however much they love it. So, it's important to remember that this can be disappointing and difficult for them and not try to cajole them into it. They may return to it another time of their choosing when they do not feel pressurized.

If possible, it is also helpful to explain to family and teachers that something your child may have enjoyed one day may not be the case the next. Sometimes adults can feel hurt or disappointed that an activity they had planned to do with your child is now not happening, so remind them that it is not personal and is part of the child's demand avoidance.

As adults, we need to be as flexible as we can be to this. Share an interest alongside your child and enjoy it with them for as long as it lasts.

Another tricky aspect alongside this can be impulsivity; you may find that your child might suddenly have a very unrealistic idea or expectation that they request from you.

Even when the requests are completely unattainable it is important not to show shock or outrage. Often the request reflects your child's need to feel in control. Your child is saying 'Can you fulfil this completely impossible request for me?' because as well as needing to feel in control they need to know that you are there to support and comfort them when they are feeling anxious and out of control. By engaging and showing a genuine interest in these impulsive demands you can make your child feel supported and heard. This also helps your child to learn about decision making by balancing up pros and cons.

Sometimes it can be really positive for your child to see you indulge an impulse they have as it may show them that you are flexible too and in turn this will help decrease their controlling behaviour.

My daughter will often have a night-time burst of energy, just at the time we are winding down from the day, and despite our tiredness she will have this last hurrah. If we are able to help her burn this energy off it is much easier to get her to bed, so finding a possible opportunity that works for you and the rest of your family where you can indulge the odd impulsive episode can be really reassuring for your PDA child.

Impulsive behaviour in our house usually increases when my daughter is stressed and feels the need for more control. Being able to be her safe person who is flexible and accommodating (as much as I can be) helps her feel more secure and in turn her need to control lessens. I cannot agree to buy her something new all the time (she loves shopping online!) but we can do lots of research and she really enjoys this, or we pretend to shop online choosing our favourite trainers, pets and so on, without actually spending any money!

Back at home twenty minutes later...

Prioritizing

As parents, we are there to guide, inform, support, love and care for our children, but how does that work differently if you are parents to a child who is highly anxious?

A number of years ago, before we were aware of PDA and my daughter only had an autism diagnosis, I was really floundering as a parent. My daughter was struggling with school, they were struggling to support her and I was struggling at home too. School was putting more supports in place and my daughter was rejecting these and then at home she was having huge meltdowns.

I was overwhelmed and fraught and I wasn't sure what was for the best. I got myself into a tricky situation with dinner times; I thought it was really important that our daughter sat with us for dinner. I mean, how was she going to be a civilized and sociable adult if she didn't sit with us, eat her dinner and discuss her day, like other 'normal' families?

But once I was able to remove this and my own preconceived expectations of how I thought we should be as a family, I was able to parent how she needed me to rather than how I thought I should. For my daughter, who had spent all day at school, full of demands and expectations, the last thing she needed was to come home to her safe space to more demands. So, we let her eat on her lap, headphones on and if she is up to it she comes and joins us at the table. Dinner times are no longer fractious or explosive. We still always offer her the option of eating with us (text messaging her works particularly well!) and now she will often feel able to join us.

Home has to be the safe space to reset with very low demands.

We still offer consistency but this comes from our emotions, staying as even-tempered as we can. This is so much easier to do when you are able to see your child is doing their best and they are not behaving the way they do on purpose. Once you can see your child through an empathetic lens you will have the accepting and flexible response your child needs. You can still use collaborative approaches too.

PRIORITIZING

school
playtime
get dressed
writing   noise
teeth brushed   walking
uniform   smells   friends
assembly   quiet time

Showing your child kindness and offering even-tempered responses to their behaviour will enable you to like your child more and in turn like yourself more as a parent.

If you see your child's meltdowns as deliberate and naughty you will feel required to instil boundaries and will cause your highly anxious child to feel unsafe, which further compounds their behaviour.

Being the most consistent, level, kind and safe person you can be to your child means they come to recognize you as a 'low demand' person – someone who is even-tempered and creates an environment for them that mirrors this. This will be really important for your PDA child.

When there is a meltdown because your child is overwhelmed you have to remain calm, take time, divert attention, avoid eye contact and minimize dialogue to see this phase out until your child is calm and you can move on.

A little while later...

Consider the demands we as parents put on our child in a day? Do we need them to tidy up? Make their bed? Eat at the table? Or would a calm, less controlling child make us feel happier and more connected to them? When your child is calm, safe and connected, then by using indirect language you will be able to increase demands too.

It takes time, years even, to shed our preconceived ideas of parenting, to reassess what we think is important, and to change our behaviour to become even, calm and consistent. All this will be individual to your family and family dynamic or even work commitments, but thinking about all these elements and what will work for you and your family is really important. When we remove unnecessary demands, our children become less combative. They have autonomy and security. And, guess what? My daughter actually offers to brush her teeth at bedtime now because we've stopped asking her!

Remember that saying, 'Pick your battles'? What is important? If they are safe, not a danger to themselves or others, then what do they need to do? What does it matter if they don't do something? It is tough to do this; as parents, 'what will people think' is inbuilt in us but if your home is happier, calmer and safer, who cares?

Positives

It is easy to spend lots of time thinking about how different our children are. There are reminders everywhere – when we stand at the school gates or talk to other parents, when we spend time around other children or even watch portrayals of families on TV. We shouldn't compare ourselves to others but it is hard not to see the differences when there are reminders all around us.

There are also the daily difficulties our children – and we – face when navigating school, home life, family and our own relationships. Family members may struggle to comprehend or appreciate how our lives are impacted on a daily basis. Even friends with well-meaning advice can be off the mark or might struggle to quite get it.

We understand how it might be for these onlookers too; it is not easy for people to understand that our children are not straightforward and can be complex and different. Unless they are living in our homes, it is really hard to see what a juggling act it is. Our lives carry daily uncertainty while we try and remain flexible to our children's needs; it is difficult for us to make plans and to have anything definite in place as we may have to change things according to how our PDA child is on the day.

When we are having meetings about our children we often have to discuss all the difficulties we are having, highlighting the negatives to try and get the right support for our children. There can be little space to talk about the positives when we are seeing and discussing their difficulties and differences regularly.

We also worry about the future: How will they manage, what will they do when they are older? Will they go to college? Live away from home? And, again, there are so many reminders, especially with social media, of all those milestones of our friends' and family's children. We've all sat down after a long day and evening of settling our PDA child and looked on social media to see a picture of our friends away for a whole weekend without their children, and seethed with envy!

This is why it is so important to see the positives of your PDA child and to enjoy them for who they are. Feeling resentful or disappointed after comparing your family life to others is never going to be helpful. As the old saying goes, 'We never know what is going on behind closed doors'. No one's life is perfect or without stress or worry, it's just that our lives are different.

All our children have their unique and lovely ways of being, and with the right support it helps us to see them for who they are. I feel genuinely proud of my daughter, I love her differences, and I think these qualities and her ability to view the world differently will be a valuable and imaginative contribution to the world, whatever way she chooses to be part of it. For example, my daughter has an amazing memory and ability to problem solve that is way beyond my capabilities.

Humour is a big part of our home too. It works effectively in supporting your child with PDA, and they will often have a great sense of humour too. My daughter is a brilliant mimic and can get the key characteristics of someone after only meeting them for a short amount of time.

"POSITIVES"

My daughter watches people and absorbs every nuance of them, noticing things about someone other people might miss, grasping mannerisms and tone of voice very quickly. This makes her a brilliant impressionist. Her insight into people also means she is a good judge of people who are relaxed and natural around children and in return it is a great honour to be someone she wants to spend time with. The chosen few get to really enjoy a chatty and funny person.

Spending and enjoying time with your PDA child means you will get to share their passions and loyalty too. I love being able to share in my daughter's witticisms about people and her shrewdness.

Your child may also be creative with an amazing, alternative view of the world as well as a vivid imagination.

They may invent new, funny games to play or characters. Let them lead you where it goes and play along with them. These other worlds may give them great comfort and help them to make sense of the world too.

All these funny and interesting parts of your child allow you to enjoy your time with them for who they are, to see beyond the diagnosis and to connect with them around their strengths and interests. Genuinely enjoying time with them is true acceptance of who they are and they will know this too, as a PDA child is excellent at recognizing when people are being honest and wanting to spend time with them.

They are also really good independent learners and will take themselves off exploring an interesting topic or project for hours when they are engaged. This can be fascinating to watch and the level of involvement and time they can commit to something when they are interested is extraordinary.

Whenever my husband has been asked about having a child with autism/PDA he always says, 'She's just her', and I love this: she is just his daughter and that is all he sees. Our children do have PDA, they are highly anxious, they require a lot of us and more, and their favourite word is probably 'no', but they are who they are and with us supporting them, and adapting the environment, not expecting them to be someone they are not, they can be who they are meant to be.

Self Care

Being emotionally consistent, funny and laid back will help your PDA child feel safe and regulated, but being all of these things all of the time can be hard work on ourselves. In fact, it's unrealistic. We can aspire to be these things but we are all human beings with our own needs and emotions, and being on an even keel for our children all the time can be exhausting.

It is really hard to always be emotionally consistent for your child and it is completely normal to grumble on occasion. Looking after a child with complex needs requires a lot from us as well as a few sacrifices along the way.

This is why it is so important to have regular breaks, however brief, so that you do not feel resentful and you can restore and repair yourself and in turn be better at looking after your child.

I also work from home now and so I don't see many people

day to day and most of my time is spent with my daughter. I am happy to make many of these sacrifices as the pay-off has been a happier and calmer child at home, but I still need to do things that are important to me. Some days I crave adult company and adult conversation, so I try and make a concerted effort to arrange this, as I know I am a happier person when I have had a break.

Neglecting our own intellectual or emotional needs can be unhealthy, and too much self-sacrifice makes us resentful or unhappy. Sometimes it can almost feel easier not to go out but it is good to try, even when we are tired, because it is a great livener to be ourselves and talk about other things that stimulate and interest us.

❤:Self Care:❤

Being our children's place of safety and support means they will need a lot of our time, so it is important to make time for ourselves. We spend so much of our energy making sure our children's needs are met, but it is important to think about our own too. What are the things that make you feel like you?

Doing the things you love will make you feel like you again, having the break you need and time to invest in your own interests. Whether that's going out as a couple for some food, a coffee with friends or an afternoon nap, sometimes just little things can make a big difference. It can also be really a good way to put things in perspective – if you've had a tough day, there is nothing like thrashing things out with a friend or partner.

Walking the dog is one of my daily breaks...

I can have an uninterrupted chat on the phone...

Or a chat with the neighbours

Taking this time and enjoying every minute (even if it's only 20 minutes!) will help you feel like yourself and in turn feel happier and less resentful when you are overstretched. Even knowing you have a small amount of time when they are watching TV or on their phones to watch a TV show or read a book will make a difference. I remember the advice after having a baby was 'sleep when they sleep' and it is not dissimilar, so take your opportunity when you can, and enjoy it. Don't spend it doing boring chores; use the time to indulge in something relaxing for yourself.

After all, if you are deregulated you won't be able to regulate your child. If you feel harassed, under pressure or as if you haven't had enough time to yourself, you will be cranky.

But it is also really important to remember that being stressed, feeling overwhelmed and being cross are all completely normal too and we all have days like this. It is not possible to feel altruistic, considerate and kind all the time. We will be snappy or impatient and we will get things wrong. We cannot ever do it right all the time and we will have other stresses and worries beyond our control. Sometimes I explain this to my daughter and say, 'I'm sorry I am grumpy today, I am tired.'

This is also a good opportunity to demonstrate our fluctuating emotions to our child and it is at these times we can show them the rationale behind them.

This is why catching up with other adults can be a great re-lease for those days when you feel you have been a useless parent.

It is also important for our other relationships with our part-ners, other children, family and friends. They want to spend time with us and it is important not to forget these other peo-ple in our lives, giving these people time to enjoy our company.

Childcare can be difficult to arrange too. In our house, our daughter struggles with being left with most people, which means we can't always do social events, especially if both of us want to go. So we have to wait until our choice of two childcare options is available and this can be tricky. Some-times I find it hard to let go and I have to remind myself that the person who is looking after my daughter might not do it quite how I do and that's okay because she will survive. I know that my child will definitely not go to bed until I get home, but that is okay too because I will have had a break and some time to myself.

And finally, find some other parents of PDA children (social media is great for this) because even though you have friends and family to support you, no one – and I mean no one – gets it like another PDA parent!

Telly? Drawing? Reading?

Five minutes later